IT'S TIME TO EAT LOQUAT FRUIT

It's Time to Eat
LOQUAT FRUIT

Walter the Educator

Silent King Books
A WhichHead Entertainment Imprint

Copyright © 2024 by Walter the Educator

All rights reserved. No part of this book may be reproduced in any manner whatsoever without written per- mission except in the case of brief quotations embodied in critical articles and reviews.

First Printing, 2024

Disclaimer

This book is a literary work; the story is not about specific persons, locations, situations, and/or circumstances unless mentioned in a historical context. Any resemblance to real persons, locations, situations, and/or circumstances is coincidental. This book is for entertainment and informational purposes only. The author and publisher offer this information without warranties expressed or implied. No matter the grounds, neither the author nor the publisher will be accountable for any losses, injuries, or other damages caused by the reader's use of this book. The use of this book acknowledges an understanding and acceptance of this disclaimer.

It's Time to Eat LOQUAT FRUIT is a collectible early learning book by Walter the Educator suitable for all ages belonging to Walter the Educator's Time to Eat Book Series. Collect more books at WaltertheEducator.com

USE THE EXTRA SPACE TO TAKE NOTES AND DOCUMENT YOUR MEMORIES

ically loaded.
LOQUAT FRUIT

It's time to eat, come gather near,

It's Time to Eat
Loquat Fruit

The loquat fruit is finally here!

Golden yellow, round and sweet,

A tasty snack that's hard to beat.

High in the tree, it loves to grow,

With leaves that shimmer in sunlight's glow.

Pick it gently, don't let it fall,

A little care, and you'll have it all.

Peel back the skin, it's silky and thin,

A treasure of flavor awaits within.

Take a bite, oh, what a treat!

The juicy loquat is good to eat.

Its taste is bright, both tart and sweet,

A fruity dance that's hard to beat.

Tiny seeds are hidden inside,

Spit them out and set them aside.

It's Time to Eat
Loquat Fruit

The birds and bees all love it, too,

Sharing the joy of the loquat's hue.

But this one's yours, go on, enjoy!

It's nature's gift for every girl and boy.

It's full of goodness, soft and ripe,

The perfect snack for any type.

From little hands to grown-up plates,

The loquat fruit always creates great tastes.

So next time when you see the tree,

With golden fruit that's hanging free,

Remember this: it's time to eat!

The loquat fruit is oh-so-sweet.

Gather 'round with smiles so wide,

Enjoy the flavors that bloom inside.

A sunny fruit, a yummy delight,

It's Time to Eat
Loquat Fruit

The loquat makes the day feel bright!

So munch and crunch, don't wait too long,

Sing the loquat's fruity song.

From tree to table, fresh and neat,

It's time to eat loquat fruit!

Eat it fresh, or bake a pie,

Loquat treats will make you sigh.

Share with friends, it's fun to do,

It's Time to Eat
Loquat Fruit

A little fruit, a lot of you!

ABOUT THE CREATOR

Walter the Educator is one of the pseudonyms for Walter Anderson. Formally educated in Chemistry, Business, and Education, he is an educator, an author, a diverse entrepreneur, and he is the son of a disabled war veteran. "Walter the Educator" shares his time between educating and creating. He holds interests and owns several creative projects that entertain, enlighten, enhance, and educate, hoping to inspire and motivate you. Follow, find new works, and stay up to date with Walter the Educator™ at WaltertheEducator.com

www.ingramcontent.com/pod-product-compliance
Lightning Source LLC
LaVergne TN
LVHW010623070526
838199LV00063BA/5254